SUPPORTING DYSLEXIC LEARNERS IN THE CLASSROOM

SUPPORTING DYSLEXIC LEARNERS IN THE CLASSROOM

{ Claire Harvey }

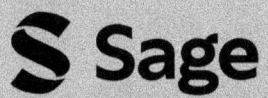

1 Oliver's Yard
55 City Road
London EC1Y 1SP

2455 Teller Road
Thousand Oaks
California 91320

Unit No 323-333, Third Floor, F-Block
International Trade Tower
Nehru Place, New Delhi – 110 019

8 Marina View Suite 43-053
Asia Square Tower 1
Singapore 018960

Editor: Amy Thornton
Editorial assistant: Harry Dixon
Production editor: Sarah Sewell
Marketing manager: Lucy Sofroniou
Cover design: Wendy Scott
Typeset by: C&M Digitals (P) Ltd, Chennai, India

© Claire Harvey 2026

Apart from any fair dealing for the purposes of research, private study, or criticism or review, as permitted under the Copyright, Designs and Patents Act, 1988, this publication may not be reproduced, stored or transmitted in any form, or by any means, without the prior permission in writing of the publisher, or in the case of reprographic reproduction, in accordance with the terms of licences issued by the Copyright Licensing Agency. Enquiries concerning reproduction outside those terms should be sent to the publisher.

Library of Congress Control Number: 2025940859

British Library Cataloguing in Publication data

A catalogue record for this book is available from the British Library

ISBN 978-1-0362-0648-2 (pbk)

ers
TABLE OF CONTENTS

About this Book vii
About the Series ix
About the Author xi
Note xiii

1 Introduction to Dyslexia and Supporting Learners 1

2 A Multisensory Approach to Teaching 13

3 Appropriate Language and Resources 21

4 Supporting Reading and Reading Comprehension 29

5 Supporting Spelling and Writing 43

6 Gaining Automaticity 57

7 Boosting Self-Esteem, Confidence and Metacognition 65

Resources for Teaching 77
References 81
Index 83

{ ABOUT THIS BOOK }

All teachers are teachers of learners with neurodivergence, including dyslexia. With some simple adjustments and accommodations, learners with dyslexia can thrive in classrooms. This book brings practical advice to teachers on how to support the learning of dyslexic learners. The strategies, methods and resources in this *Little Guide* will support the learning of all children.

- Authored by an expert in the field
- Easy to dip in and out of
- Interactive activities encourage you to write into the book and make it your own
- Fun and engaging illustrations throughout
- Read in an afternoon or take as long as you like with it!

Find out more at
www.sagepub.co.uk/littleguides

{ ABOUT THE SERIES }

A LITTLE GUIDE FOR TEACHERS series is little in size but big on all the support and inspiration you need to navigate your day-to-day life as a teacher.

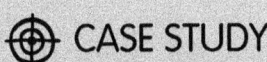 **CASE STUDY**

 **REFLECTION**

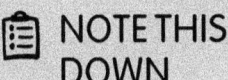 **NOTE THIS DOWN**

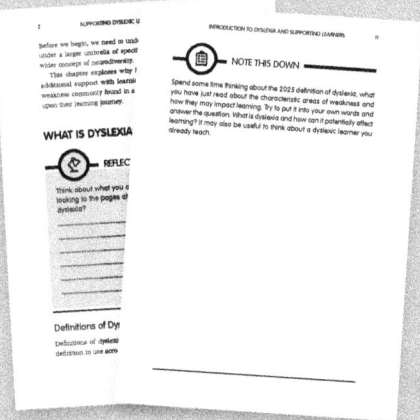

www.sagepub.co.uk/littleguides

ABOUT THE AUTHOR

Claire Harvey has worked at the Helen Arkell Dyslexia Charity since 2017. She is passionate about making a real difference to the lives of individuals with dyslexia. As Head of Education, she is responsible for the consistently high quality of educational content on dyslexia. The Helen Arkell Dyslexia Charity has a reputation in the sector as the 'gold standard' provider of training on dyslexia. Claire oversees training for educational professionals to become specialist teachers as well as other training.

Claire is involved in events and training opportunities, including national dyslexia conferences. She also delivers presentations to schools and parent organisations to share best practice, top tips and useful teaching strategies and resources.

Claire has worked in a large primary school as SEN Team Leader responsible for assessing mainstream pupils, identifying those in need of additional support, allocating them to appropriate intervention groups, teaching the weakest learners herself and closely monitoring all pupils' progress.

The Helen Arkell Dyslexia Charity supports people with dyslexia to bring about positive changes in their lives. Since 1971, we have been removing barriers to learning and life for children, young people and adults with dyslexia and other specific learning difficulties by providing expert, personal and life-changing support.

Following our founder Helen's mantra, to help people regardless of their ability to pay, we provide free support to many individuals from lower-income backgrounds.

Together we inspire people to believe in themselves, achieve their goals and succeed on their own terms.

The Helen Arkell Dyslexia Charity website: https://helenarkell.org.uk

NOTE

Some individuals with dyslexia favour being referred to as **learners with dyslexia**, feeling the 'person' comes before the difficulty. Other learners may prefer **dyslexic learner**, embracing their dyslexic profile as a key part of who they are. Throughout this book, to acknowledge both variations in terminology, the author will use both these terms.

It is important when considering how best to support dyslexic learners to do this in light of their age and stage of development.

CHAPTER 1
INTRODUCTION TO DYSLEXIA AND SUPPORTING LEARNERS

This chapter explores:

- Definitions of dyslexia
- Definitions of specific learning difficulties and neurodiversity
- Characteristic areas of difficulty in dyslexia
- The potential impact of these difficulties on learning

Before we begin, we need to understand what dyslexia is, how it sits under a larger umbrella of specific learning difficulties and an even wider concept of neurodiversity.

This chapter explores why learners with dyslexia may require additional support with learning and how characteristic areas of weakness commonly found in a dyslexic learner's profile may impact upon their learning journey.

WHAT IS DYSLEXIA?

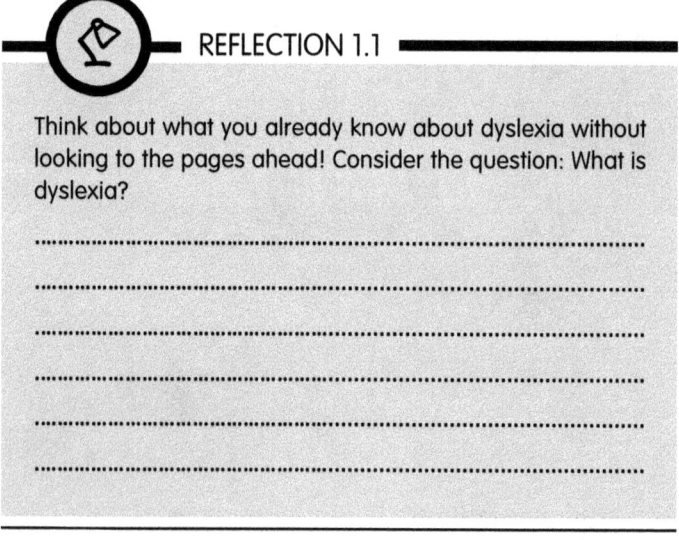

REFLECTION 1.1

Think about what you already know about dyslexia without looking to the pages ahead! Consider the question: What is dyslexia?

....

....

....

....

....

....

Definitions of Dyslexia

Definitions of dyslexia have changed over time and there is no one definition in use across the world. However, following over two years of work by a group of expert panel members, a consensus definition of dyslexia was agreed in 2025. It is as follows:

- Dyslexia is a set of processing difficulties that affect the acquisition of reading and spelling.
- In dyslexia, some or all aspects of literacy attainment are weak in relation to age, standard teaching and instruction, and level of other attainments.
- Across languages and age groups, difficulties in reading fluency and spelling are a key marker of dyslexia.
- The nature and developmental trajectory of dyslexia depend on multiple genetic and environmental influences.
- Dyslexic difficulties exist on a continuum and can be experienced to various degrees of severity.
- Dyslexia can affect the acquisition of other skills, such as mathematics, reading comprehension or learning another language.
- The most commonly observed cognitive impairment in dyslexia is a difficulty in phonological processing (i.e. in phonological awareness, phonological processing speed or phonological memory). However, phonological difficulties do not fully explain the variability that is observed.
- Working memory, processing speed and orthographic skills can contribute to the impact of dyslexia.
- Dyslexia frequently co-occurs with one or more other developmental difficulty, including developmental language disorder, dyscalculia, ADHD, and developmental coordination disorder.

Carroll, J., Holden, C., Kirby, P., Snowling, M. J. & Thompson, P.A. (2025)

WHAT ARE SPECIFIC LEARNING DIFFICULTIES AND NEURODIVERSITY?

REFLECTION 1.2

Think about what you already know about specific learning difficulties and neurodiversity without looking to the pages ahead! Consider the question: What are specific learning difficulties and neurodiversity?

....

....

....

....

....

....

Specific Learning Difficulties and Neurodiversity

Dyslexia sits alongside other conditions that affect learning. The umbrella term for these conditions is 'specific learning difficulties'. These conditions may affect how an individual receives, processes and recalls information. It is a difference or difficulty with particular aspects of learning. Dyslexia is a specific learning difficulty. Examples of other specific learning difficulties are developmental co-ordination disorder (also known as dyspraxia), dyscalculia and dysgraphia.

- Developmental co-ordination disorder (DCD) is a condition affecting fine and/or gross motor co-ordination and movement, and sequencing.
- Dyscalculia is a difficulty with numeracy – learners having difficulty understanding basic number concepts, lacking an intuitive grasp and sense of numbers and struggling to learn number facts and procedures.
- Dysgraphia refers to severe problems with handwriting, as a result of weak underlying fine motor skills. Dysgraphia is also thought to interfere with other aspects of writing such as generating the content, the sequencing of ideas, punctuation, grammar and spelling.

Specific learning difficulties, including dyslexia, are also examples of neurodiversity. The term neurodiversity recognises normal variation and differences in brain function that occur naturally across the human population. It is a recognition that we all have neurological differences. Specific learning difficulties and other conditions like ADHD (attention deficit hyperactivity disorder), ASC (autistic spectrum condition) and DLD (developmental language disorder) all lie under this wider term of neurodiversity.

- ADHD is a neurobiological condition with three main symptoms of impulsivity, hyperactivity and inattention. These symptoms can impact many areas of daily life as well as learning.
- ASC, also known as ASD (autism spectrum disorder), presents with impairment in three main areas: social communication, social interaction and social imagination. It is a lifelong developmental disability which affects how people communicate and interact with the world.

- DLD is a speech and language disorder where language skills are much weaker than non-verbal abilities. Those with DLD may have difficulties with receptive language (understanding spoken language) or difficulties with expressive language (generating language themselves) or both.

The Neurodiversity Umbrella

- ADHD (attention deficit hyperactivity disorder)
- ASC (autistic spectrum condition)
- DLD (developmental language disorder)
- SpLDs:
    - Dyscalculia
    - Dyspraxia
    - Dysgraphia (developmental co-ordination disorder)
    - Dyslexia

Each neurodiverse condition has its own specific features, but they can overlap and often a learner may have more than one. One study has estimated that 70% of dyslexic learners experience additional difficulties linked to other neurodiverse conditions, many severe enough to warrant an additional diagnosis (Muter, 2021). And we need to be mindful of this – the chances of a dyslexic learner having a second specific learning difficulty or neurodiverse condition is high, co-occurrence is common and dyslexia existing in isolation is less common.

DYSLEXIA: WHAT ARE THE CHARACTERISTIC AREAS OF DIFFICULTY?

The definition of dyslexia proposed by Carroll et al. (2025) refers to dyslexia as 'a set of processing difficulties'. It expands to clarify that primarily these 'processing difficulties' are phonological in nature.

In essence, difficulties with phonological processing, the processing of sounds in language, is a key characteristic of dyslexia.

Examples of phonological processing skills include:

- **phonological awareness** – an awareness of small sounds (phonemes) in words, and an ability to accurately identify sounds, discriminate between similar sounds and manipulate these sounds
- **phonological processing speed** – an ability to make sense of and generate language-based information accurately and efficiently
- **phonological memory** – an ability to identify accurately, retain briefly and recall efficiently sequences of sounds
- **phonemic decoding skill** – use the knowledge of letter/s–sound relationships to sound out and read words

The definition of dyslexia also acknowledges that phonological difficulties 'do not fully explain the variability that is observed'. There are additional processing difficulties that are commonly observed in dyslexic learners' profiles.

Examples of additional processing difficulties (listed in the definition) include:

- **working memory** – the ability to hold information in short-term memory whilst manipulating and doing something with it
- **processing speed** – an ability to efficiently take in, interpret, understand and respond to information the brain receives
- **orthographic skills** – the ability to retrieve and form letters, letter sequences and spelling patterns when writing

Some people, when asked to describe dyslexia, may mention words moving on the page, words blurring or merging together, confusing similar looking letters or words, experiencing glare from the page, and difficulties tracking and keeping place when reading. It is true that some learners with dyslexia, but certainly not all, may experience some visual difficulties in addition to difficulties associated with their dyslexia. But visual difficulties *are not* a characteristic of dyslexia and do not appear in the definition as a defining feature. Any visual difficulties need to be explored further by a suitably trained visual specialist.

DYSLEXIA: WHAT IS THE POTENTIAL IMPACT ON LEARNING?

The definition of dyslexia indicates that dyslexia can affect 'all aspects of literacy attainment' and often attainments 'are weak in relation to age'. That is, in comparison to peers of a similar age and stage, dyslexic learners' attainments may be lower. Specifically, difficulties with 'reading fluency and spelling are a key marker of dyslexia'. Dyslexia commonly impacts upon both reading and spelling skills. And whilst most dyslexic learners do, with appropriate support and intervention, eventually develop accuracy in their reading and spelling skills, very often the journey is lengthier and more effortful than for more neurotypical learners.

The impact of dyslexic difficulties may be more apparent in relation to fluency, especially in the long term. Dyslexic learners may achieve a level of accuracy in their reading and spelling skills, but their fluency, their level of automaticity in these skills, may continue to be impaired into later years and adulthood.

Dyslexia will impact different learners in different ways at various points of their academic journey and life. The definition states that 'dyslexic difficulties exist on a continuum and can be experienced to various degrees of severity'. Some learners will experience more profound difficulties in primary school as they learn foundational literacy skills; others may experience more difficulty in secondary school with a greater number of subjects and more independent learning required. Some may compensate well at school, have sound coping strategies, respond well to support and intervention, but may struggle in higher and further education as the demands of the curriculum increase.

The potential impact is much wider than just literacy attainment. The definition indicates that dyslexia 'can affect the acquisition of other skills, such as mathematics, reading comprehension or learning another language'. In reality, due to the wide range of processing skill deficits, the impact is more far-reaching, affecting not only learning in all classroom subjects but all aspects of everyday learning and life skills.

Given the significant areas of weakness discussed previously, it is not surprising that many learners with dyslexia experience low self-esteem and/or lack confidence at some stage in their life, very commonly in the school years when so much of what they are asked to do is effortful for them. These children are making a huge effort to achieve what many other children achieve seemingly effortlessly, and that makes it frustrating for them. However, there is a growing movement to recognise positive attributes of dyslexic individuals.

Linking Characteristic Areas of Difficulty to Impact

Below are some examples of how some of the characteristic areas of difficulty may impact on specific areas of learning.

Weak Phonological Awareness

- Trickier to learn phonic code and map sounds onto letters (reading)
- Trickier to learn phonic code and map letters onto sounds (spelling)

Slower Phonological Processing Speed

- Longer to read words on the page and draw meaning from the words
- Longer to arrange thoughts and formulate sentences
- Longer to spell words

Weak Phonological Memory
- Trickier to represent all sounds when spelling
- Trickier to hold onto and blend sounds when reading longer unfamiliar words

Weak Phonemic Decoding Skills
- Difficulty blending (combining sounds) together to read words
- Difficulty segmenting (separating sounds) in words to read longer words with multiple parts
- Difficulty recognising common patterns in words

Weak Working Memory
- Difficulty remembering instructions accurately
- Difficulty concentrating for extended periods
- Taking longer to complete tasks
- Difficulty working independently, staying on track
- Harder to get thoughts on paper with accurate punctuation, sentence structure, grammar, etc.

Slower Processing Speed
- Longer to complete tasks, especially under the pressure of time (e.g. in examinations)
- Difficulty following instructions, directions and routines
- Longer to process numerical information (e.g. recall number facts and mathematical procedures)

Weak Orthographic Skills
- Weaker recall of common spelling patterns in words
- Slower to recognise common words or parts of words when reading

# NOTE THIS DOWN

Spend some time thinking about the 2025 definition of dyslexia, what you have just read about the characteristic areas of weakness and how they may impact learning. Try to put it into your own words and answer the question: What is dyslexia and how can it potentially affect learning? It may also be useful to think about a dyslexic learner you already teach.

CHAPTER 2
A MULTISENSORY APPROACH TO TEACHING

This chapter explores:

- What is multisensory teaching?
- Why use a multisensory approach?
- How to integrate multisensory approaches into the classroom

Using a multisensory approach to teaching – using techniques and resources that allow for learning to occur through auditory, visual and kinaesthetic modalities – will not only ensure a range of learners' neurodiverse learning preferences are being met but will also deepen the learning experiences of all learners in the classroom. If a learner can engage all their senses as they learn, make learning more of a whole brain exercise, the content becomes more memorable and the likelihood of transfer of new knowledge to the long-term memory increases.

You may feel that you already incorporate some multisensory teaching into your classroom, but are you really using a full range of multisensory learning techniques in each lesson? There may be room for expansion and improvement.

REFLECTION 2.1

Spend a couple of minutes thinking about what you already know about multisensory teaching and if you feel you already incorporate multisensory teaching techniques or resources into your teaching. Try to do this without looking to the pages ahead! Consider the question: What multisensory teaching techniques or resources do I currently use?

....

....

....

....

....

....

WHAT IS MULTISENSORY TEACHING?

Multisensory teaching is not a new concept. In the early 1900s Maria Montessori based her work on observations of children and experimentation with the environment, materials and lessons available to them. She noted how children learnt best when they used all their senses and she developed a teaching method and a range of teaching materials to reflect this. Augur, a dyslexia activist and champion of multisensory teaching, described multisensory learning as 'learning by the simultaneous use of the eyes, ears, speech organs, fingers and muscles' (Augur, 1985). Multisensory teaching involves using teaching techniques and resources that allow for learning to occur through auditory, visual and kinaesthetic routes.

WHY USE A MULTISENSORY APPROACH?

All learners are neurodiverse. Part of this natural variation means that they will all learn differently, process tasks differently, have different learning styles, learning preferences and strategies to learn effectively. By teaching in a multisensory pattern, encouraging learners to engage all their senses in the learning process, you will be much more likely to meet the needs of all the learners in your classroom, no matter what their individual learning preferences are.

Furthermore, by teaching to engage all senses, you are more likely to make good use of individual learner's strengths, which will compensate for any areas of weakness.

The more senses, or modalities, a learner uses as they learn, the more engaged the learner becomes in the process of learning and the deeper the learning experience will be. If a learner can engage their visual (seeing) sense, auditory (listening) sense and kinaesthetic (using movement and touch) sense as they learn, the learning experience will be more intense and more memorable. Because multisensory learning involves more pathways in the brain, this is also likely to aid the transfer of new knowledge to long-term memory.

Paying one 'visit' – or repeated similar 'visits' – to a learning objective may be memorable in the short term, but to truly embed learning, doing so in a variety of ways, engaging more senses and making learning more of a holistic experience, is much more effective in the long term. If we revisit any new learning in a variety of ways and use all our senses, and we reinforce and overlearn the new material, then in future we are much more likely to be able to recall the new knowledge automatically from our long-term memory. That new learning pathway has been set securely.

HOW TO INTEGRATE MULTISENSORY APPROACHES INTO THE CLASSROOM

Facilitate learning by not only structuring the lesson carefully but also by teaching in a multisensory fashion and integrating as many senses as possible into your choice of teaching methods and resources. This way you can teach once and be more likely to meet all the needs of all your learners, with all learners being given an equal chance to learn.

Using Visual Methods

To make learning more of a visual experience, to stimulate visual pathways, consider some of the following suggestions:

- **Colour** is important – encourage learners to add colour to content through the use of highlighters to underline, and coloured pencils and pens to annotate. Experiment with colour coding and linking types of information with a certain colour.
- **Coloured paper and post-it notes** can also help to add more visual appeal.
- Encourage learners to **draw pictures to illustrate new facts and concepts**, as they will undoubtedly have a picture in their

head that works for them. It is often said that *one picture is worth a thousand words*. For example, draw a character from a book to bring them to life.
- **Create colourful displays** like collages using pictures and text to build a strong visual image.
- Encourage learners to **create diagrams and flow charts** of how facts and concepts relate to each other. For example, create a cartoon-like story board to recall the plot/story line/timeline.
- Supplement school topics with **video** to help make content more memorable and generate a strong visual memory.
- Consider using a **practical demonstration** wherever possible so a learner can see something with their own eyes.

Using Auditory Methods

To stimulate auditory pathways, to encourage learning through listening and talking, consider some of the following suggestions:

- Can learners **make up rhymes or raps** about their work? For example, to help with number bonds to ten use 'eight and two on my shoe' and 'seven and three having a cup of tea'.
- **Listening to audio books** can be a very effective way for learners to engage with a story.
- Some learners will embed new learning more securely if they **repeat out loud** new facts or even sub-vocalise under their breath.
- **Use technology** that allows text to be spoken aloud to add sound.
- Could learners verbally **record their notes and play them back** ? Hearing content in their own voice can be very effective.
- Encourage periods of **collaboration** where learners can talk through key lesson elements with their peers, helping each other to process and secure new concepts.

- **Mnemonics** can work very well to remember information. For example, remembering how to spell 'said' through the mnemonic 'space aliens in danger'.

Using Kinaesthetic Methods

To make learning a more kinaesthetic experience, to encourage learning with and through movement and touch, consider some of the following suggestions.

- Can learners wherever possible **do things practically**: touch, feel and learn by receiving physical feedback?
- Try to **use games and movement**. For example, can learners walk around the classroom reading key facts on post-its placed around the room, or discovering hidden facts? Something as simple as this – integrating movement – can help.
- Use **manipulatives and props** to demonstrate new concepts – for example, rods or blocks to support maths concepts, and wooden or magnetic letters to support reading and spelling.
- Try writing key facts to learn on **coloured cards**, maybe attached on a keyring, so learners can hold them – this tactile element helps as it is more interactive than just reading them off a page.
- **Standing up and moving away from the desk** periodically can help to keep learners engaged and make the learning more memorable – make good use of corridors and playgrounds.

 NOTE THIS DOWN

Spend some time thinking about multisensory teaching and all you have read in this chapter. Think about expanding your range of multisensory teaching techniques and resources. Answer the question: What new multisensory teaching techniques or resources can I integrate in my lessons to make learning more holistic and memorable by engaging visual, auditory and kinaesthetic pathways?

CHAPTER 3
APPROPRIATE LANGUAGE AND RESOURCES

This chapter explores:

- What is the most appropriate language?
- What is the most appropriate presentation style for written resources?
- Suggestions for how to integrate these into the classroom

The language and resources used in the classrooms need to be dyslexia friendly. Some simple adjustments to how information is presented can significantly improve the accessibility and engagement, not only for learners with dyslexia but for all learners.

Some adjustments and accommodations can reduce potential barriers to learning and support dyslexic learners to access content and make the intended progress. Some very simple modifications to language and resources can aid and promote the learning of dyslexic children.

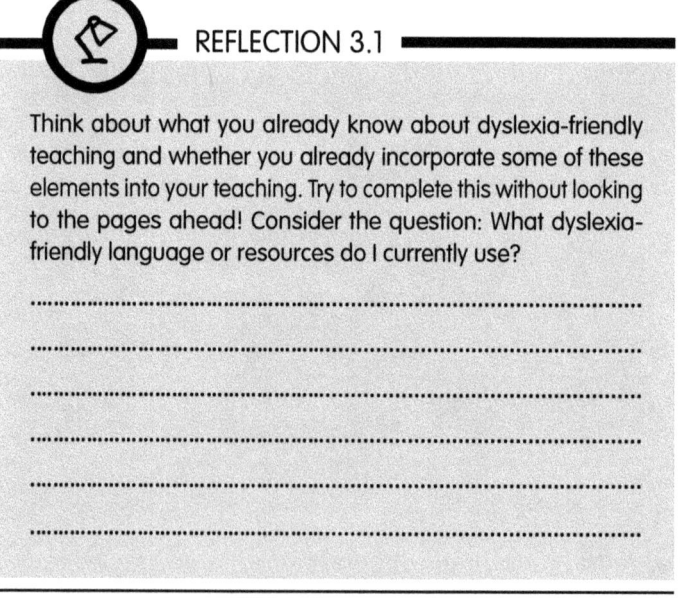

REFLECTION 3.1

Think about what you already know about dyslexia-friendly teaching and whether you already incorporate some of these elements into your teaching. Try to complete this without looking to the pages ahead! Consider the question: What dyslexia-friendly language or resources do I currently use?

....
....
....
....
....
....

WHAT IS APPROPRIATE LANGUAGE?

The most appropriate language in the classroom will allow your message to be delivered clearly with the content accessible to all the learners in your classroom, including those with dyslexia. As discussed previously, dyslexic learners with a slower speed of phonological processing may take longer to process language, longer to make sense of what they hear and longer to generate their response to what they hear. Dyslexic learners may also have a weaker working memory and find it difficult to process a lot of information at one time and there may be a risk that they lose certain elements of the content.

Teachers need to be mindful of these difficulties. However, the good news is that there are some very simple adjustments that can be made to the language used in the classroom which could lessen the impact of these difficulties. Talking at the right pace to allow learners to process what is being said and formulate their responses can help. Knowing when to be silent is also key. Keeping instructions simple and sequential can help. The use of signal words to structure the content and highlight key elements can be very successful. Trying to not assume learners have fully understood what has been taught and getting into the habit of checking can be worthwhile. Be prepared to repeat yourself and be open to exploring alternative ways of explaining something. Finally, try to use positive language wherever possible.

Using Appropriate Language

Consider some of the following suggestions:

- **Slow down** – Speak more slowly. This will help learners to make sense of the content.
- **Allow for thinking time** – Try to count to three (in your head) after you have said something (and before you move on) or after you have asked a question. This will allow your learners time to process what you have said, giving them valuable thinking time.
- **Don't talk when learners are busy** – Try to stop talking when your learners are busy working on a task, especially if

they are writing. Talking when they are concentrating might interrupt their train of thought and overload their working memory (which is busy with the task in hand).

- **Keep instructions simple** – Try to give instructions using simple language. Shorter sentences are preferable to more complex ones. Speaking in the active voice rather than the passive voice is also more easily understood. For example, 'the dog chased the cat' rather than 'the cat was chased by the dog'. The subject of the sentence does the action rather than being acted upon by the verb. Avoid idioms, sarcasm and double meanings when giving instructions as these can 'distort' the message.

- **Keep instructions sequential** – Give instructions in the order that you would like them to be done. Instructions are less likely to be confused and more likely to be memorable for dyslexic learners if they are delivered sequentially. For example, 'Please finish the question you are on and then put your books away and line up by the door' rather than 'Line up by the door but first finish the question you are on and remember to put your books away.'

- **Break complex tasks into a series of smaller steps** – By breaking more complex tasks into a series of smaller, more manageable steps or 'chunks' of activity, dyslexic learners are more likely to achieve success and less likely to feel overwhelmed or miss an important element of the task.

- **Use signal words** – Consider using some signal words to help alert learners to key points in your message and to support their understanding of the content and the relationship between certain elements of what you are teaching. For example:
    - There are three things to remember…
    - The first… The second…
    - Most importantly…
    - Finally…
    - Let's summarise…

- **Check understanding** – Check you have been understood by all your learners. You want to be sure that they are clear on the learning objective and what they have been asked to do. Very often we feel we have been clear but there may be some in your classroom who need further clarification. You could ask learners to turn to a peer sitting nearby and discuss together (either the instruction or the learning just delivered). You could ask some learners to rephrase the learning or instructions, although this must be done discreetly not to draw undue attention to any difficulties.
- **Be prepared to repeat yourself or explain in a different way** – Be open to repeating and explaining again if needed. This might involve exploring alternative ways of explaining something. Remember the multisensory methods discussed in Chapter 2 and consider if there is a more visual or kinaesthetic route to making your message clearer. For example, if you are explaining an activity that follows, you could show your learners a WAGOLL (what a good one looks like) so they can see what they are working towards as well as listening to you explain the task. Or when teaching a new concept, you could show a video, film or pictures to supplement your explanation.
- **Use positive language** – Use positive language wherever possible and look to highlight what your learners have done well so far and the progress they have already made.

USING AN APPROPRIATE PRESENTATION STYLE FOR WRITTEN RESOURCES

There are some simple adjustments to how written documents are presented in the classroom that can vastly improve accessibility, reducing potential barriers that might make the content trickier to read and process.

Consider some of the following suggestions for how to modify the presentation of documents (or presentation of content on smartboards) used in the classroom:

- **Use a dyslexia-friendly font** – Use a font that is simple to read, that has easily recognised, clearly formed letters, which are less likely to be confused with other similar looking letters. Examples are **Verdana**, Arial, Comic Sans, Trebuchet, Calibri and Aptos. There are also specialist fonts available with weighted letters like Open Dyslexic.
- **Use a large enough font size** – Use a font size of at least 12–14 points to improve readability.
- **Avoid underlining and italic** – If you wish to highlight some of the text, it is better to use the bold function as underlining and italic can make it look as though the letters are running into each other, which reduces readability.
- **Use appropriate line spacing** – Wherever possible, increase line spacing to at least 1.5 so the lines of text are distinct.
- **Always left justify the text** – It is much easier to read text when it is left justified and the spacing between words is even. Fully justified text creates uneven gaps between words, causing jerky eye movements and making the text more difficult to read.
- **Avoid block capital letters** – It is harder to read words in block capitals and dyslexic learners are more likely to recognise words in the more familiar lower case. So, use capitals when appropriate but try to avoid using BLOCK CAPITALS unnecessarily.
- **Consider using non-white paper** – Some learners with dyslexia find reading text on white paper harder than on non-white paper. It can be worth experimenting with different coloured paper to see if readability increases. However, an alternative to printing on non-white paper (which may be more costly for schools than white) is to use muted or softer black text. This can be achieved by reducing the black font to 85% black.

 CASE STUDY – TOM

Tom, a Year 7 learner, was diagnosed with dyslexia in Year 6. For a number of years previously, he struggled with written tasks. His teacher noted that Tom often found it tricky to get started with any written tasks in class, was often unclear on what was required of him, struggled to work independently and his written work did not match his very able verbal skills. His teachers implemented some adjustments to support his learning needs. Key adjustments included adapting how any verbal instructions were given to Tom about written work with particular attention to keeping these simple and using some signal words. For example:

> First I would like you to sketch a brief plan about the story… then I would like you to write the introduction… and then the main part, followed by the conclusion. Finally, I would like you to proofread what you have written.

This helped to break down written tasks into a number of manageable steps that were written on a card next to Tom as a reminder. He was also shown examples of what a finished piece of writing was likely to look like. Teachers regularly checked with Tom that he understood written tasks and whether he had any questions, and they provided specific, positive, verbal feedback to him on his completed writing tasks. As a result of these changes, Tom's confidence in his writing skills grew significantly and his teachers noticed that he was able to work more independently, improve the quality and write more.

 NOTE THIS DOWN

Spend some time thinking about dyslexia-friendly language and resources and all you have read in this chapter. Think about how you might modify your language and/or the presentation of written resources used in the classroom. Make a list of some changes you would like to make in the coming weeks. Think about what could be done immediately and what might need some more time and planning to implement.

CHAPTER 4
SUPPORTING READING AND READING COMPREHENSION

This chapter explores:

- How to support phonological awareness
- How to support early reading skills and the relationship between letters and sounds
- How to support the development of reading skills and encourage independence
- How to support reading comprehension, including skimming and scanning

The development of reading skills starts before entry into school with phonological awareness – an awareness of sounds and how sounds can be manipulated to form words. Phonological awareness underpins the acquisition of reading skills. In primary school, children learn to read. They learn to match the sounds to letters, strings of letters and whole words. In secondary school, learners are then expected to read in order to learn and are exposed to a wider array of subjects and related vocabulary. There is more emphasis here on reading comprehension, understanding what they have read.

At all stages of this process, as discussed in Chapter 1, learners with dyslexia may struggle to acquire these skills and may require specific support.

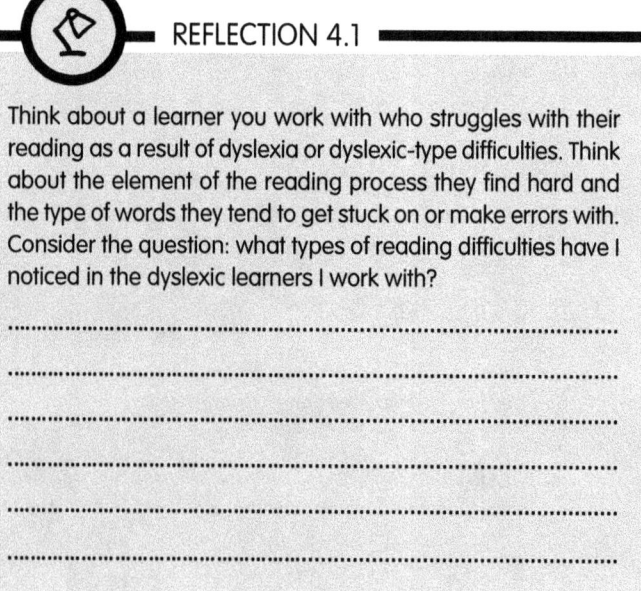

REFLECTION 4.1

Think about a learner you work with who struggles with their reading as a result of dyslexia or dyslexic-type difficulties. Think about the element of the reading process they find hard and the type of words they tend to get stuck on or make errors with. Consider the question: what types of reading difficulties have I noticed in the dyslexic learners I work with?

....

....

....

....

....

....

HOW TO SUPPORT PHONOLOGICAL AWARENESS

If you work with young learners in Key Stage 1, or even in early Key Stage 2, you may notice they have less developed phonological awareness. Phonological awareness, discussed in Chapter 1, is a phonological processing skill, and is often weak in dyslexic learners. These learners may lack an awareness of the small sounds – phonemes – in words, struggle to accurately identify the sounds, find it tricky to discriminate between similar sounds and to manipulate these sounds. Weak phonological awareness can hamper learning to read and for some learners explicit teaching to support phonological awareness may help.

Supporting Auditory Discrimination

Encourage learners to be aware and detect the difference between similar sounds in words. This is all about playing with sounds in words verbally and helps to form clear representations that each letter or letter pattern has a distinct sound. These skills are needed when learning to read.

- Can they clap when they hear a single letter sound like /t/ amongst other sounds like /p/ /g/ /f/ /t/? Repeat for all letter sounds.
- Can they clap when they hear the same sound at the start of words, or in the middle of words or at the end of words? Repeat for all letter sounds.
- Some sounds can be very tricky as they sound very similar like /f/ /th/ /v/ and /m/ /n/ and children might need practice in isolating them. Discuss what makes these similar sounds different – for example, the position of the mouth and tongue when the sounds are made.

Rhyme

Encourage learners to notice when words rhyme and to make up their own rhyming words. This helps to form analogies between sound patterns and written patterns in words. If a learner can read 'flock', they can read 'tock' and 'clock' with the same final sound and letter pattern.

- Teach nursery rhymes or read rhyming books
- Play rhyming games like Rhyme Soup – 'I'm making a soup, and the ingredients are socks, rocks, blocks', etc.

Segmentation

Encourage learners to break words into smaller parts, to isolate the different sounds and create smaller chunks. Manipulating sounds in words is utilised when learning to read.

- Ask if they can hear what the two syllables are in a compound word like 'snowman'.
- Can they identify the first sound in words like 'pin'? (/p/). Then the middle sound in words like 'jump'? (/u/). Then the final sound in words like 'smash'? (/sh/).

HOW TO SUPPORT EARLY READING SKILLS AND THE ACQUISITION OF PHONIC AWARENESS (THE RELATIONSHIP BETWEEN LETTERS AND SOUNDS)

All children need to learn the phonic code – to match, phonically irregular words, the letter sounds (phonemes) to the corresponding letters (graphemes), to decode and read a large number of decodable words. This starts with matching sounds to single letters and then blends of letters and strings of letters. In addition, learners need to recognise and read phonically irregular words or 'sight words' that cannot be decoded.

Many dyslexic learners take longer to learn both phonically regular words and sight words. They tend to need more exposure to both the letter patterns and the whole words before these are securely banked in their long-term memory and recalled with a level of automaticity as they read. Supporting the reading of regular words and the reading of sight words can be extremely valuable. The aim is for learners to achieve both accuracy **and** fluency with reading skills through repetition, over-learning and regular reinforcement.

Supporting the Reading of Regular Words

Learners need to be aware of the sound every letter of the alphabet makes, the sound for every blend of letters (e.g. 'tr'), for every consonant digraph (e.g. 'sh') or vowel digraph (e.g. 'ou') and for every string (e.g. 'ing'). If they are familiar with the sound of all phonic patterns, they can attempt to read phonically regular words. If some of these are not familiar, or perhaps not recalled automatically and with ease when reading, then the following could be considered:

- **Make a set of letter/sound link cards** with the letter on one side and a picture of an object starting with the sound on the reverse and practise seeing the letter, saying the sound, then turning over the card and saying the prompt word. For example, /mm/ 'mug'. Practise little and often till these are all recalled easily.
- **Make a note of any unfamiliar patterns and practise reading a whole word family** containing that pattern. For example, if 'ou' that makes the sound /ow/ is tricky then practise with 'pound', 'found', 'ground', etc. 'Precision teaching' sheets with lots of target words for learners to read as quickly

as they can every day can work well. Free templates for worksheets and reading games can be found on websites like Worksheet Genius.

Even when learners with dyslexia are familiar with all the phonic patterns, they may still struggle to read longer, unfamiliar words and to apply this phonic knowledge. They may have (as explored in Chapter 1):

- difficulties with phonological awareness
- weak working memory
- weak phonological memory
- weak phonemic decoding skills.

These common characteristics of a dyslexic profile can weigh heavily on a learner with dyslexia's ability to read longer words and can lead to guessing words rather than carefully breaking the word into parts, identifying the separate sounds and then blending the sounds together to say the word. These learners would benefit from being taught a 'word attack strategy' for how to decode longer words. *Toe by Toe: A Highly Structured Multi-sensory Reading Manual for Teachers and Parents* by Cowling and Cowling (1993) outlines some useful 'word attack' strategies. More information about this resource is included later in this chapter.

Supporting the Reading of Irregular Words

There are many words that cannot be sounded out using phonics, cannot be decoded, as there is little correspondence between the letters and the sounds. Sometimes referred to as 'sight words' or 'common exception words', these need to be practised regularly and committed to memory before they can be recalled with ease when reading. Some dyslexic learners find they need more practice with these words to achieve the level of automaticity required to see the word and immediately recognise and read it. A search for the *First 100 High Frequency Words* and the *Next 200 High Frequency Words* will generate lists of these words.

Supporting learners with dyslexia to read these irregular words can be key as they are thought to make up around 30% of all prose read. Familiarity with them can boost reading accuracy, fluency and confidence. The following methods for learning irregular words are worth considering:

- Identify any unfamiliar words and work on three or four at a time until they can be easily identified and read accurately. TAs and parents can support this process. Aim for the words to be read as a single word and then practise reading them in phrases, and then in sentences and finally in longer passages of prose.
- Discuss the appearance of the word, its meaning, and how it can be used in a sentence to provide context. This will help 'bank' each word to memory.

HOW TO SUPPORT THE DEVELOPMENT OF READING SKILLS AND ENCOURAGE INDEPENDENCE

When the reading of regular and irregular words becomes more accurate, and learners have built up their knowledge and skills, many dyslexic learners may continue to lack fluency and confidence in reading. Supporting the further development of reading skills, aiming for a greater level of independence reading and enjoyment of reading are the next step. Following the principle of the Matthew effect, good readers get better at reading with increased experience and exposure and a cumulative advantage emerges. The following methods and resources can support the development of reading skills for learners with dyslexia:

- As reading skills develop, **closely monitor the books** dyslexic learners are encouraged to read. When reading for pleasure, high interest books will appeal more to reluctant readers. Closely assess the difficulty level of books. If the text is too tricky and more than one word in ten is unknown to the reader, consider dropping down a level.
- Consider providing a **dyslexia-friendly range of reading books**. Some publishers offer books presented in a dyslexia-friendly font and layout, printed on off-white paper, and content matched to the age of the reader regardless of their reading ability.
- **Regularly listening** to dyslexic learners read aloud will allow you to monitor their reading skills as they develop.
- Encourage developing readers to become more independent readers and to **build up their self-monitoring and self-correction skills.** For example, if they are stuck on a word and they have tried to decode unsuccessfully or are not familiar with the word, encourage them to read on to the end of the sentence and see if some clues emerge from the sentence context or grammar. If mistakes are made reading, try to give the learner time to self-correct, either immediately or at the end of the sentence. Questions like 'Does that sound right to you?' and 'Would you like to re-read that sentence again?' help to promote self-monitoring and self-correction skills.
- The **use of assistive technology** can boost reading skills – for example, any text-to-speech application that reads text aloud from a website, word document, e-reader, text file or pdf. For many dyslexic learners, with emerging reading skills, text-to-speech applications allow more challenging texts to be accessed independently, giving them opportunities that their peers have. It also exposes them to a rich and varied vocabulary and key curriculum subject-related terminology. Reading along whilst hearing the text spoken aloud (ideally with each word highlighted as it is read aloud) will also increase the likelihood

of their recognising and reading these words independently in future. The British Dyslexia Association's Technology website lists a variety of text-to-speech options.

- **Reader pens** can work well for dyslexic learners. A reader pen, when scanned over a word or sentence, will read the text aloud. As with text-to-speech applications, reader pens increase the likelihood of recognising and reading these words on subsequent occasions, removing a potential barrier. Reader pens may also be considered in examination settings.
- **Audio books** allow a set published text to be read aloud to a learner. Some are purely audio, and others include text and audio. A wide range of books are available as audio books, including curriculum texts. Many learners find listening to set texts from an audio book supports their reading development as they become more familiar with the language, characters, themes and plot development. Audio books can also foster a love of reading and entice even the most reluctant reader to pick up books and further develop their reading skills.
- **Paired reading, shared reading and repeated reading** can all improve reading accuracy and fluency. Dyslexic learners could be encouraged to 'pair up' with stronger readers in class for paired reading. Paired reading has a 'substantial impact' on accuracy (Lavan and Talcott, 2020). In paired reading, the two learners (or an adult and a learner) read together out loud. The stronger reader therefore reads the words the weaker reader cannot. The weaker reader repeats any words the stronger reader provides. At times the weaker reader reads alone, but the stronger reader returns if needed. This promotes greater fluency and more expression when reading. Research behind paired reading, videos and instructions are readily available online. Shared reading is, as it suggests, where readers take turns reading paragraphs or pages and again is thought to improve reading fluency, expression, enjoyment and engagement.

Many dyslexic learners will improve their own reading skills by re-reading a text for a second time. The second read is often more accurate, more fluent, read with greater expression and a deeper understanding extracted from the text.
- **Pre-learning of curriculum words** can be very effective. Ahead of introducing a new topic, dyslexic learners could be provided with a list of related words. Any time spent either in small groups with TAs or at home with parents supporting the reading of these words (including the meaning), greatly benefits these learners and improves their access to the forthcoming content.

HOW TO SUPPORT READING COMPREHENSION, INCLUDING SKIMMING AND SCANNING

The good news is that reading comprehension is likely to improve as reading accuracy and fluency develop. There may be more 'space' in the working memory to consider the meaning of the text when less effort is being expended on the mechanics of reading.

However, many dyslexic learners will struggle with aspects of reading comprehension as a result of the characteristic areas of difficulty commonly seen in a dyslexic profile and discussed in Chapter 1 (weak working memory, slower speed of phonological processing). These areas of difficulty may weigh more heavily as learners move towards the end of primary school and transition to secondary school and beyond where the emphasis moves from learning to read to reading to learn. A greater number of subjects, more advanced vocabulary and concepts, alongside expectations of more independent learning all increase the complexity of reading comprehension demands.

There are some strategies and resources that can support the development of reading comprehension skills, and you may wish to consider the following:

- **Paired reading** was discussed earlier in relation to developing reading accuracy and fluency. In paired reading, the content is discussed periodically. This style of reading, because less effort is being expended decoding tricky words, is thought to leave more capacity to comprehend the text.
- **Skimming** a passage of non-fiction text before starting to read can strengthen comprehension. Encourage learners to skim through the passage and note the title, subheadings, pictures and read the first and last sentences. This is about looking for clues as to what the passage is about and thinking, 'What do I already know about this topic?' Priming the brain on the topic before reading, increases the chances of the text being more easily understood when read.
- **Scanning** a text to find specific answers to reading comprehension questions may need to be taught explicitly. Teach the following six simple scanning steps:

1. Read the question.
2. Underline the key part of the question.
3. Consider what the answer might look like (a date, a name, an adjective, an emotion, contains a certain word, etc.).
4. Scan the text to find the answer (not reading) with your finger sweeping back and forth across the lines.
5. Find the answer and read the sentence it appears in.
6. Go back to the question and check whether this answers it.

- Teach learners to read comprehension questions carefully. The **BUG method** works well to ensure that key elements of the question have been identified. The B is for **Box the command word**/s e.g. describe, explain, state, suggest, compare, contrast. The U is for **Underline the key words**. The G is for **Go over the question again and think about what it is asking for.**

CASE STUDY – SALLY

Sally, a Year 5 learner, is experiencing dyslexic-type difficulties. Specifically, Sally struggles with reading and reading comprehension, frequently saying that she does not enjoy reading. Her teacher notes that Sally often finds it tricky to read longer, unfamiliar words and resorts to guessing or missing these words as she reads aloud. As a result, Sally's reading comprehension is weak, and she often struggles to answer questions on texts she has read. Her teacher implements some reading and reading comprehension support for Sally to support her learning needs. Sally is taught a word attack strategy and is encouraged to break longer, unfamiliar words into smaller chunks and blend them together to read. She is also encouraged to stop and re-read any sentence where she feels she may have misread a word. Sally's reading accuracy and fluency improves, and her reading comprehension improves as a result. Sally can glean much more from the text and consequently her reading enjoyment improves. She is also taught a scanning strategy to look specifically for any answers to reading comprehension questions she can not immediately recall from memory. Teaching staff regularly listen to Sally read, monitoring her word attack skills, her self-correction skills and her improving reading comprehension skills. Sally's confidence grows significantly and her teachers notice that she begins to enjoy reading for pleasure.

 **NOTE THIS DOWN**

Spend some time thinking about how to support reading accuracy and fluency and all you have read in this chapter. Think about how you might support dyslexic learners in your classroom to develop their reading skills. Make a list of some changes you would like to make in the coming weeks. Think about what could be done immediately and what might need some more time and planning to implement.

CHAPTER 5
SUPPORTING SPELLING AND WRITING

This chapter explores:

- How to support early spelling skills
- How to support the development of spelling skills and encourage independence
- How to support writing skills

Spelling and writing skills are possibly the trickiest skills for a dyslexic learner to master. At all stages in the process of developing spelling and writing skills, as a result of the characteristic areas of weakness that lie within a dyslexic learner's profile discussed in Chapter 1, learners with dyslexia may struggle with elements of spelling and writing, and may require specific support.

SUPPORTING SPELLING

English is a problematic language when it comes to spelling with so many different influences on spelling patterns over the many centuries of its development.

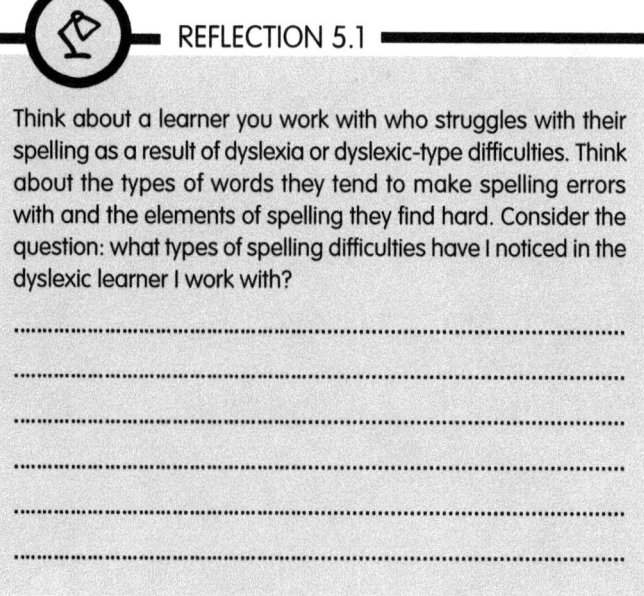

REFLECTION 5.1

Think about a learner you work with who struggles with their spelling as a result of dyslexia or dyslexic-type difficulties. Think about the types of words they tend to make spelling errors with and the elements of spelling they find hard. Consider the question: what types of spelling difficulties have I noticed in the dyslexic learner I work with?

....

....

....

....

....

....

There are regular words, words that are spelt as they sound and irregular words, where there is little phoneme/grapheme (sound/spelling) correspondence. And some spellings are governed by rules that need to be learnt like 'i before e except after c'.

In primary school, children learn to spell. They learn to match sounds to letters and strings of letters and they learn to spell more irregularly spelt words. Phonological processing skills are often weak in learners with dyslexia. Specifically, weak phonological awareness and weak phonological memory may weigh heavily and impact spelling phonically regular words. Weak working memory, weaker orthographic skills and a slower processing speed may also affect learning to spell. Some learners will benefit from more targeted support to acquire spelling skills.

Spelling Regular Words

Children need to be able to write every letter of the alphabet to represent each sound, to spell two or more letters that blend together (e.g. 'bl' or 'spr'), to spell digraphs (e.g. 'th' or 'ch'), to spell vowel digraphs (e.g. 'ai' or 'ee') and for every string (e.g. 'ought'). If they are familiar with the spellings for the sounds of all the phonic patterns, they can attempt to spell phonically regular words.

If some of these are not familiar, or perhaps not recalled automatically and with ease when writing, then the following tips may support **the spelling of phonically regular words** (where there is correspondence between letters and sounds):

- Look for words that contain the same phonic pattern and can be taught together. Once a link between a sound and the corresponding spelling pattern has been made, try to expand and teach the family of words that contain the same pattern. This strengthens the link between the sound and the spelling pattern and extends spelling knowledge.

- Wherever possible, discuss the sound that letters and letter patterns make, alongside the spelling letter pattern. Strengthening the memory of the sound can help, especially with learners who then go on to subvocalise (say the sound under their breath) as they spell. Subvocalising as phonically regular words are spelt can be an effective support strategy for many dyslexic learners.
- Encourage learners to think about the sounds heard in words, to segment (break up) longer words into smaller chunks and to represent these sound chunks with corresponding letters. Phoneme frames can be effective to support this process. Ask 'What sounds do you hear?' /sh/ /ip/ /ment/ and these sounds are spelt 'sh' 'ip' 'ment'.

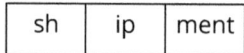

Figure 5.1 'shipment' phonemes

Spelling Irregular Words

Many words cannot be spelt by recalling phonic patterns. These irregular words – 'sight words' or 'common exception words' – must be practised regularly and committed to memory before they can be spelt with ease. Some dyslexic learners with a weak working memory find they need more practice with these words to achieve the level of automaticity required to spell the word when they are writing a sentence.

The following tips may be considered to support the spelling of irregular words (where there is little correspondence between sounds and letters):

- Look for a memorable method to teach the spelling. For example, a mnemonic for a word like 'said' could be 'space aliens in danger'. Or a story about the letters for a word like 'necessary' could be 'it is necessary for a shirt to have one collar and two sleeves' – there is one 'c' and two 's's in this word. Or saying the word in the way it is spelt could help for words like 'Wed – nes – day' and 'fri – end'. Or perhaps there is a word within the word like 'hat' in 'what' or 'hen in 'when'. Some spellings can become part of a picture like the word 'look' where two eyes can be drawn in the middle letters.

- Irregularly spelt words are likely to need much more practice until they are secure. Chapter 2 included ideas on how to bring a multisensory approach into learning to support dyslexic learners. Multisensory methods work particularly well for learning spelling – for example, rainbow writing (writing the letters in a word over and over again in different colours whilst saying the letter names). A spelling window, available from the Helen Arkell Dyslexia Charity is designed to do just this, enables reinforcement of spellings using a multisensory approach. It can be used in the classroom as a multisensory alternative to look–cover–write–check.
- When practising spelling irregular words, some learners will naturally subvocalise (speak under their breath). This can be useful, but with irregular words, encourage the use of letter names, not sounds, because the sounds are not helpful here (and may be confusing) with little correspondence between letters and sounds in irregular words.

Spelling Words that Follow Rules

Some spellings are governed by a particular rule. Rules need to be learnt in order to spell a variety of words that follow that rule.

The following tips support the spelling of words where there is a rule to learn:

- Look for words where the same rule governs the spelling and can be taught together. Once a link between a spelling rule and the corresponding spelling pattern has been made, try to expand and teach the family of words that follow this rule. This strengthens the link between the rule and the spelling pattern and extends spelling knowledge. For example, 'i before e except after c' guides the spelling of receive, perceive, deceive, but also believe, reprieve, achieve, relieved.
- Encourage learners to 'discover' spelling rules themselves. Many learners enjoy being detectives and uncovering spelling rules. Encourage this process with questions like 'What do you notice about these words?'

Developing Spelling Skills and Encouraging Independence

Towards the end of primary and moving into secondary school, learners are expected to spell a wider range of words and to use these when writing to demonstrate their understanding and knowledge in an array of subjects and related vocabulary. However, many dyslexic learners experience ongoing spelling difficulties and will benefit from continuing support to develop these skills.

If spelling difficulties linger beyond primary school, there is a risk that weaker spelling skills may start to have more impact on a learner's choice of words when writing; they may not use words that they are unable to spell, words that do in fact lie within their lexicon and knowledge base. Considering bypass strategies at this stage may be wise in order to reduce the negative impact that weak spelling skills may have upon a learner's ability to demonstrate their knowledge and understanding of the curriculum in written format and their resulting attainment. Using bypass strategies will also promote independence, reduce reliance on an adult to provide spellings, whilst allowing for the continuing development of spelling skills.

The following tips may support **the development of spelling skills and promote independence**:

- Increasing awareness of affixes (prefixes and suffixes) and teaching the spelling of these affixes can develop spelling skills. If root words can be spelt correctly and then a variety of affixes accurately applied to the root words, then a single accurately spelt word becomes an exponential number of correctly spelt words. For example, 'help' can become helpful, unhelpful, helpfulness, unhelpfulness, helpless, helping, helplessly, etc.
- Many learners find that creating a personal spelling journal supports development of their spelling skills. Encourage learners to note any tricky words to spell in a small booklet. They could add any curriculum-related words to the journal, and they could add some favourite descriptive words that lie in their oral vocabulary. Encourage learners to add to this journal frequently and to use the journal when writing in class to support spelling.
- Pre-learning of curriculum words can be very effective. Ahead of introducing a new topic, dyslexic learners could be provided with a list of related words. Any time spent either in small groups with teaching assistants or at home with parents supporting the spelling of these words (including the meaning), greatly benefits these learners and improves their ability to write on the forthcoming content.
- Many learners with dyslexia report that using a word processor is not only easier and more efficient than handwriting (if touch typing skills are faster than handwriting skills) but that spelling difficulties are less likely to interfere with their thought processes. When typing with predictive and corrective text

enabled, a tricky or incorrect spelling is flagged, and learners can be supported to correct it, thereby reinforcing knowledge of the correct spelling.
- For many dyslexic learners with emerging spelling skills, speech-to-text applications allow a script with rich and varied vocabulary and key terminology related to curriculum subjects to be generated through dictation and speech recognition. If learners proofread these scripts, they are then exposed to the correct spelling, which supports development of skills.
- Assistive technology may also be used to provide the spelling of key words whilst handwriting. There are a variety of apps that will give learners a tricky spelling when dictated.
- A dyslexia-friendly spelling dictionary may also be of use in the classroom. The words are arranged in alphabetical order based on the initial sound in target words rather than the correct spelling, thereby allowing words like photograph to be looked up under /f/.

Supporting Writing

Writing involves not just spelling but also generating, ordering and linking ideas, constructing sentences and then paragraphs, writing in a number of styles, using appropriate grammar and punctuation, employing a wide variety of descriptive language, and mastering either handwriting or word processing skills. Weak phonological processing skills, alongside weak working memory, and a slower processing speed, discussed in Chapter 1, may impact the development of writing skills, making transferring all the wonderful ideas that lie in the mind of a dyslexic learner onto paper trickier. Some learners will benefit from more targeted support to acquire and hone their writing skills.

REFLECTION 5.2

Think about a learner or two that you work with who struggle with writing as a result of dyslexia or dyslexic-type difficulties. Think about the element of writing they find hard. Consider the question: what types of writing difficulty have I noticed in the dyslexic learners I work with?

....

....

....

....

....

....

The following tips may support **writing skills**:

- Some learners with dyslexia struggle to generate ideas, particularly in creative writing tasks. They may benefit from learning a strategy that helps them to get started and move off the blank page stage. A simple memorable strategy like **'who, where, what, why, when'** works well to help with the development of initial ideas. These question words can be linked with the five fingers on their hand as an aide to memory.
- Encouraging a planning stage before writing can benefit all learners, but especially dyslexic learners. If the content and sequence of ideas can be decided ahead of the writing phase,

then more working memory and processing capacity can be channelled into the other elements of writing (e.g. choice of language, spelling, grammar, sentence arrangement and punctuation). There are a multitude of planning tools to help structure the process of planning. For learners at primary school age, bullet points written on sticky notes notes work well, as do story mountains (a method of visually planning the plot and structure of a story linked to a mountain shape with set stages of an opening, a build-up, a climax, a resolution and an ending) or a six-point plan. For older and more able learners, mind maps, flow charts or a Lotus diagram (a method of visually planning writing by expanding on a central idea into a matrix of surrounding boxes) can help arrange not only the structure of a piece of writing but also some of the key details to be included.

- Some learners will find it helpful to use a word processor as discussed above.
- Even when a planning method has been used, some younger dyslexic learners may struggle to structure their sentences, and older learners may struggle with paragraph formation. For younger learners, teach the grammatical elements of a good sentence (subject, verb, object) explicitly. For older learners, devise a strategy for paragraph formation – for example, a hamburger (or sandwich) paragraph where each paragraph has a top piece of bread (the introductory sentence of the paragraph), some meat, cheese or salad middles (the supporting sentences of the paragraph) and a bottom piece of bread (the final summarising sentence of the paragraph which may link to the next paragraph).
- When writing skills are developing, and grammar, punctuation and spelling are not yet automatic, appropriate scaffolding can provide the support many dyslexic learners need at this stage.

A useful analogy is that these learners may need to use 'training wheels' for a while, to practise new skills before they cycle on their own without them. Examples of effective scaffolds for writing in class are:

- a word mat or list of WOW words
- a reminder of all necessary elements of punctuation like a punctuation pyramid
- a list of sentence starters to bring variety to the opening of sentences and/or to make a link to a previous sentence
- a list of connectives to support the formation of complex sentences and the use of clauses
- and a list of topic- or curriculum-related words to support their use and spelling.

- All learners benefit from learning how to proofread a piece of completed writing. Dyslexic learners often make simple errors that are relatively easy to detect and they should be encouraged to proofread their work and self-correct. The first step is to help learners be more aware of the types of error they commonly make so they know what they are looking for – for example, missing capital letters or full stops, spelling errors with common homophones, or very long sentences overusing a certain sentence starter or the same connective. The second step is to encourage reading the script from beginning to end (forwards), preferably out loud or under their breath, and learners asking themselves, 'Does it make sense? Is the punctuation correct?' The third step is to skim for spelling errors starting at the end and moving towards the start (backwards), word by word, learners asking themselves, 'Is this word spelt correctly?' These proofreading checks can be integrated into usual classroom practice.

CASE STUDY – DAN

Dan is a Year 7 dyslexic learner with strong verbal ability that is not reflected in his written work, mainly due to persistent spelling difficulties. He avoids using complex vocabulary that lies within his oral lexicon, and he makes errors with high-frequency, irregularly spelt words. His teacher implemented some spelling support for Dan to support his learning needs. Dan was able to use a tablet in class with spell-checking tools and a speech-to-text function. He was also supported to create a personal spelling journal that contained all his favourite descriptive words, many high-frequency words and some subject-specific words. As a result of these changes, Dan's spelling ceased to restrict his written work and hamper his ability to demonstrate his knowledge and understanding in a written format. His confidence grew as a result of using these bypass strategies (a personal spelling journal, speech-to-text software, word processing with spellcheck enabled) and teaching staff noted that his spelling and writing skills improved.

# NOTE THIS DOWN

Spend some time thinking about how to support spelling and writing and all you have read in this chapter. Think about how you might support dyslexic learners in your classroom to develop skills. Make a list of some changes you would like to consider making in the coming weeks. Think about what could be done immediately and what might need some more time and planning to implement.

CHAPTER 6
GAINING AUTOMATICITY

This chapter explores:

- **Why dyslexic learners may take longer to achieve automaticity**
- **How to support automaticity**

Automaticity is the ability to perform a task without having to think about it consciously. Some learners will move swiftly from the stage of having to think consciously about a new skill to the next stage of achieving automaticity and almost unconsciously using that new skill – for example, from learning a spelling, to using the word in their writing without having to stop and think about how it is spelt. Dyslexic learners are likely to need more practice, more repetition, more overlearning before new skills become automatic.

REFLECTION 6.1

Think about a learner with dyslexia or dyslexic-type difficulties you work with who appears to need more overlearning and more practice before newly taught skills are secure and they can demonstrate automaticity. Think about how they differ from more neurotypical learners you work with. Consider the question: what have I noticed about automaticity in the dyslexic learners I work with?

....

....

....

....

....

....

....

WHY DYSLEXIC LEARNERS MAY TAKE LONGER TO ACHIEVE AUTOMATICITY

Many learners with dyslexia have difficulty achieving automaticity with new skills taught in the classroom. They may need to more consciously complete tasks in class, compared to their peers who may be able to complete these tasks more unconsciously. Dyslexic learners can learn skills and strategies to combat their areas of difficulty but they may never become automatic with some skills. Or they may need much more practice than a neurotypical learner before something becomes automatic for them.

A lack of automaticity with new tasks is something that many education professionals and researchers have observed as characteristic of dyslexia. The definition of dyslexia (Chapter 1) states that 'difficulties in reading fluency … are a key marker of dyslexia'. It is here that a lack of automaticity with reading can be seen to impact reading fluency. Many dyslexic learners learn to read accurately, but many struggle to read with fluency, to read smoothly and effortlessly. They may need much more practice than their peers to read with automaticity, without conscious effort.

The definition of dyslexia (Chapter 1) outlines how difficulties with phonological processing, working memory, orthographic skills and processing speed all contribute to the problems experienced by dyslexic learners. As a result, how new information is taken in, processed and made sense of, is stored and then ultimately retrieved may all be affected. Weak working memory can make it more problematic when learning new skills, facts and processes. Working memory is where so much of what we learn is held temporarily as we make sense of it before being banked in our long-term memories, ready to be retrieved when needed. If dyslexic learners have a weaker working memory than their peers in the classroom, this has an impact on the amount of information they can process at one time. Therefore, it is not just reading that dyslexic learners may struggle to achieve automaticity with, but many of the skills taught in the classroom including reading comprehension, writing skills, spelling skills and elements of numeracy.

Weak reading comprehension is often a result of weaker reading comprehension. If decoding and reading accuracy are weak, then reading is unlikely to be fluent. And if reading skills are not automatic, and effort is being expended on accuracy, there may be little space left for reading comprehension, for absorbing the meaning of the text being read. Often dyslexic readers will need to read and then re-read a text to extract meaning; their comprehension of texts they have read is not automatic.

Many learners with dyslexia will struggle to spell with a level of automaticity. They may be able to learn a list of spelling words for a test in a given week, but without adequate practice in spelling these new words, they lack automaticity and therefore when it comes to using the words when they write, when so many other skills are required (e.g. punctuation and grammar), they make errors.

How to Support Automaticity

Dyslexic learners often benefit from teaching being delivered in smaller, more manageable chunks, not being overwhelmed with too much information in one lesson. They also need to revisit the teaching points regularly. Finally, they need plenty of opportunity to practise the new skills until they are secure. Through repetition, overlearning and repeated exposure, and practice, automaticity is more likely. The following tips may support the development of automaticity:

- **Embed at the start of lesson plans a recap** of a previous lesson's learning objective before teaching the next step. Revisiting key points of an earlier lesson will work well for the dyslexic learners in your classroom. They will respond well to frequent short recaps of previous learning.

- **Embed a plenary at the end of a lesson** and summarise the key points. Mini plenaries may also be of benefit at key stages in a lesson to recap what has been taught so far before moving on.
- If possible, provide **frequent opportunities to practise new skills**. Dyslexic learners respond well to repetition and may need more experience with a new skill than their peers.
- **Provide scaffolding** if required to support dyslexic learners whilst they practise new skills. It is better for a learner to practise the same task as their peers with a scaffold in place than to have a different task and miss out on a valuable opportunity to rehearse and embed new skills. Examples include having a personal spelling journal (discussed in Chapter 5) to hand for spelling topic curriculum words, and a text-to-speech application or reader pen (discussed in Chapter 4) to support reading accuracy whilst completing a reading comprehension task.
- It is better for a learner with dyslexia to achieve success with **smaller, more manageable 'chunks' of learning** and then be guided to extend this knowledge than to attempt to process and learn a larger amount of information in one sitting and potentially fail to hold onto any of it. For example, consider reducing the number of spellings to be learnt each week or 'rolling over' three or four of the trickier ones to the following week to allow for consolidation.
- Be mindful that for dyslexic learners there may be a big jump between understanding new information taught in class and then being able to use or demonstrate it independently and with automaticity. Some dyslexic learners reach **automaticity in steps** – for example, being able to read or spell a word at word level comes first, then in a phrase, then in a sentence and finally in a longer passage of prose. Support this process with appropriate activities for the stage they are working at.

- **Consider carefully the learning objective** for each lesson and ensure that work completed in the lesson allows all learners in the classroom to practise that key skill. This will ensure that learners with dyslexia have the opportunity to rehearse and repeat. It sounds simple, but often other elements of a task can reduce a dyslexic learner's valuable practice time. For example, try to avoid the need to copy from the board as this is tricky and effortful and will slow down the rate at which a dyslexic learner can practise the key skill (which is not copying!). Instead, provide a handout containing the content, questions or activity on it. Or, if the task is to write using descriptive language, rhetorical or literary devices, or in a particular genre, you could provide an outline of the story, as generating the ideas for the story may take up too much time and leave little time or effort for a dyslexic learner to practise the core skill.

NOTE THIS DOWN

Spend some time thinking about automaticity and all you have read in this chapter. Think about how you might support dyslexic learners in your classroom to develop automaticity, to provide the opportunity for overlearning and consolidation and to ensure new skills are secure. Make a list of some changes you would like to consider making in the coming weeks. Think about what could be done immediately and what might need some more time and planning to implement.

CHAPTER 7
BOOSTING SELF-ESTEEM, CONFIDENCE AND METACOGNITION

This chapter explores:

- Why dyslexic learners are at risk of low self-esteem and confidence
- How to recognise low self-esteem and confidence
- The potential impact of low self-esteem and confidence
- How to boost self-esteem and confidence
- How to boost metacognition

Self-esteem can be defined as confidence in one's personal abilities and is closely tied to our self-respect, self-worth, our opinions and beliefs about ourselves. We know that a learner's level of achievement, their behaviour and engagement in the classroom can be strongly influenced by how they think and feel about themselves – their self-esteem. It is not surprising that many dyslexic learners, as a result of challenges they experience with learning, may experience low self-esteem and lack confidence. They may also lack an awareness of how they learn best, what works for them – metacognition. Teaching staff play a key role in boosting the self-esteem, confidence and metacognition of all learners in the classroom, including dyslexic learners.

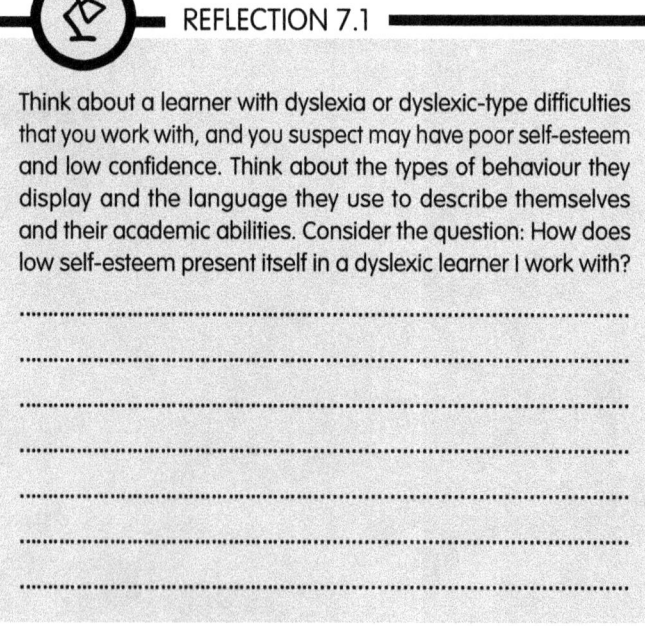

REFLECTION 7.1

Think about a learner with dyslexia or dyslexic-type difficulties that you work with, and you suspect may have poor self-esteem and low confidence. Think about the types of behaviour they display and the language they use to describe themselves and their academic abilities. Consider the question: How does low self-esteem present itself in a dyslexic learner I work with?

....

....

....

....

....

....

....

HOW TO RECOGNISE LOW SELF-ESTEEM AND CONFIDENCE

Teaching staff need to be able to recognise the warning signs of low self-esteem and confidence. There are some typical signs and signals. Not all of the following are a consequence of low self-esteem and confidence, but together a number of these can point towards it.

- Learners may be reluctant to apply themselves to schoolwork, to undertake tasks (particularly new tasks). This is often mistaken for disobedience and difficult behaviour when in fact it may be related to a lack of motivation resulting from low self-esteem and a lack of confidence to tackle a novel task.
- Learners may dislike taking risks necessary to engage in new learning. They may feel uncomfortable the first time they start a new topic or new activity or task.
- Learners may be anxious or even defensive or argumentative.
- Some learners may find the need to over-check their work and may appear worried or nervous about the standard (particularly in relation to their peers).
- Learners with low self-esteem can be pessimistic about their abilities (make negative comments about their skills).
- Some learners may find it difficult to motivate themselves.
- Other people's opinions of their strengths and weaknesses are often taken more seriously by dyslexic learners than they should be. They may appear overly sensitive to feedback from peers or teaching staff.

WHY DYSLEXIC LEARNERS ARE AT RISK OF LOW SELF-ESTEEM AND CONFIDENCE

Research suggests that learners with dyslexia, specific learning difficulties and literacy difficulties are at an increased risk of developing negative self-perceptions of themselves and their abilities as learners (Gibby-Leversuch et al., 2021) The common areas of difficulty that lie within a dyslexic cognitive profile (discussed previously in Chapter 1) can impact heavily upon their acquisition of literacy and potentially numeracy skills. A slower speed of processing, weaker memory skills, weak phonological processing skills can all hamper progress and lead to a perception that learning is hard, not enjoyable and something that is often unachievable. Additionally, as a result of processing difficulties, a dyslexic learner's attainment may follow a different growth curve, and they are going to be very aware of the difference between their current level and that of their more neurotypical peers.

We often place learners in sets, on different reading bands, on different tables within the classroom. We offer them differentiated tasks, we provide one-to-one support or interventions – all important to help them progress and access the curriculum and learn, but this will change how they perceive their own abilities, their self-esteem and confidence. They will naturally compare themselves to their peers and this can trigger a change in their feelings, in their opinion, their beliefs about their own worth.

THE POTENTIAL IMPACT OF LOW SELF-ESTEEM AND CONFIDENCE

Early experiences at home or in the school environment, where a dyslexic learner may have struggled with a task or failed to meet the level required, may be characterised by failure and have set a negative cycle in motion. Low self-esteem can lead to low confidence and even a fear of taking on any tricky tasks due to previous experiences. For some learners this becomes a lack of full engagement with learning, a reluctance to participate in the classroom. Behavioural issues may become apparent at this stage. As a result of non-engagement, attainment drops, and ultimately self-esteem can fall further, and the negative self-esteem cycle continues.

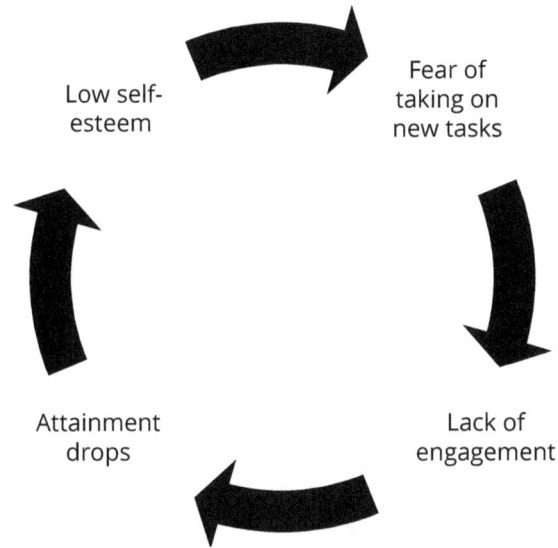

Figure 7.1 Negative self-esteem cycle

Low self-esteem can manifest in the classroom as a lack of motivation, a lack of engagement and a fear of tackling new tasks or developing skills. If unresolved, feelings of hopelessness, helplessness and worthlessness follow. You may notice learners voice the following types of comments:

- **Hopelessness**: 'There is no point trying to read this book because I won't be able to.'
- **Helplessness**: 'I can't spell this word and I don't even want to learn how to spell it.'
- **Worthlessness**: 'I just don't deserve to do well in this test. I'm stupid.'

HOW TO BOOST SELF-ESTEEM AND CONFIDENCE

The good news is that self-esteem is not inherited, it is learned, influenced by temperament yes, but mainly moulded through life experiences, influenced by feedback from peers and adults, reinforced by everyday experiences, and is therefore capable of dramatic change.

Children need to feel that that they have the ability to succeed, and positive self-esteem is part of this. They need to feel that if they put in the effort, even if things are tricky as they are for many dyslexic learners, they can reap rewards. Teaching staff can support learners with dyslexia to boost self-esteem and to keep levels high. Healthy self-esteem and confidence will lead to a willingness to tackle trickier

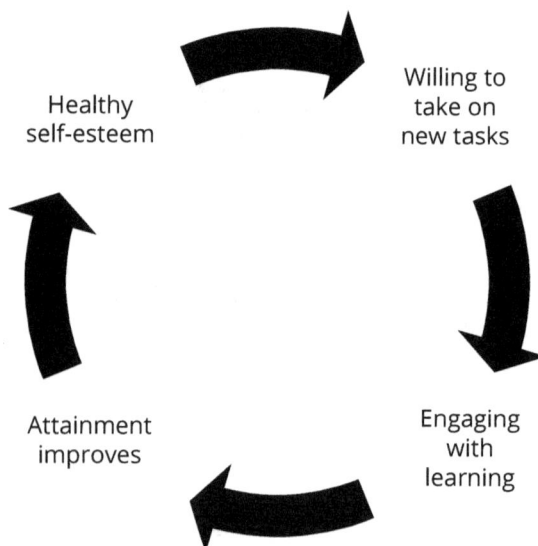

Figure 7.2 Positive self-esteem cycle

tasks, to engage with learning in the classroom, to achieve goals with attainment rising, and as a result self-esteem remains high – a positive self-esteem cycle is established.

The following strategies and tips to boost self-esteem and confidence may be useful:

- **Discuss how neurodivergent differences are 'normal' across the population.** Explain that we are all different and each have our own strengths and areas of weakness – all part of the rich tapestry of life!
- **Recognise areas of strength.** All learners, including dyslexic learners, have strengths, and learners need to know that they have stronger skills as well as relatively weaker ones. Drawing attention and celebrating these strengths will help to boost self-esteem. Strengths may lie in non-literacy areas of the curriculum like maths, design technology or science, or in extra-curricular activities like drama, sport, art, IT or music. If a dyslexic learner can achieve success with their stronger skills and feel this is recognised by teaching staff and peers, this will provide a boost to their self-esteem.
- **Ensure learners have positive experiences.** It is important that learners with dyslexia experience what it is like to succeed, to have positive experiences. This might involve finding an alternative method for learners to demonstrate their knowledge and understanding, ideally tapping into an area of strength, perhaps using visual or creative skills – for example, by using a speech-to-text application to dictate a piece of creative writing, creating a pictorial mindmap to summarise key facts on a topic, or preparing a verbal presentation on a topic. This is not always possible every day in every topic but look for opportunities for a dyslexic learner to use some of their strengths to succeed with a task.
- **Positive experiences don't have to be based within the classroom.** They may be generated outside the classroom,

in their hobbies, personal interests, clubs, etc. Encourage dyslexic learners to share these experiences with you and their peers in class and give great feedback on these accomplishments.

- **Positive feedback from teaching staff and their peers will provide reassurance to the learner of their strengths and set them up for further tasks.** Each success, no matter how small, will build self-esteem and boost confidence and provide motivation to tackle other tasks, including tasks that are trickier.
- **Set achievable targets, learning objectives and goals.** Share these targets with your learners and discuss how they will be achieved. Then measure success in relation to these and celebrate progress. This provides a real sense of achievement for the learner but also involves them in the process of learning, improving their engagement.
- **Acknowledge and reward effort as well as attainment.** This helps to foster a learning mindset and improves commitment to the process of learning.
- **When marking, give specific, positive feedback.** This should be on what they have achieved, where they have improved, as well as pointing out what needs more practice, or is not there just yet. Aim for two-thirds of marking to be positive and one third identifying the next step, the next target or learning objective.
- **A visual display in the classroom,** like a Wow Wall, works well to highlight strengths and achievements. This can include work from the classroom like a well punctuated piece of writing, or from outside the classroom like a fantastic painting in art, or a gymnastics badge from a club outside school. These are visual reminders of positive experiences, of occasions where strengths were used to compensate for areas of weakness, or where hard work and application lead to success, or where

targets/learning objectives were met, or where a talent can be celebrated.
- **Promote resilience and a growth mindset.** Create an atmosphere where learners feel safe to make mistakes and able to try again. Encourage learners to view mistakes as an opportunity to learn, to grow and improve.

HOW TO BOOST METACOGNITION

Metacognition can be defined as an awareness of the process by which learners use their knowledge, skills and strategies to learn effectively. Teaching staff have a key role in boosting metacognition by encouraging children from their earliest years to discover their own way of learning and what works best for them. For dyslexic learners, an awareness of their preferred learning style and what strategies and methods work well for them is crucial as it will support them to be effective and efficient learners, concentrating their effort on what is likely to achieve the strongest results.

For example, some learners with dyslexia will develop successful strategies like chunking longer, unfamiliar words into smaller parts to read, or using a mnemonic to recall a tricky spelling, or practising weekly spellings with a spelling window, or skimming before reading non-fiction. Some dyslexic learners will favour using one of their senses more than another when learning. For example, their auditory sense may be more active when learning and they sub-vocalise as they rehearse full sentences as they write, or as they spell or read longer unfamiliar words, or as they learn history facts. If you notice that a particular method or strategy has worked well for a learner, draw attention to it and encourage them to use this method and learning style more and in other areas of the curriculum.

This is all about guiding learners to be more independent, to take ownership of their learning, to engage with the process and understand more fully how they learn best and what works for them. Encourage learners to reflect by asking themselves some of these questions:

- How have I done this before?
- What worked well for me as a method?
- What did I find easy? Difficult? Why was that?
- Should I tackle this in the same way as before or try a different strategy?

# NOTE THIS DOWN

Spend some time thinking about self-esteem, confidence and metacognition and all you have read in this chapter. Think about how you might support dyslexic learners in your classroom to boost their self-esteem, confidence and metacognition. Make a list of some changes you would like to make in the coming weeks. Think about what could be done immediately and what might need some more time and planning to implement.

RESOURCES FOR TEACHING

Anyone Can Spell It – A Helen Arkell Dyslexia Charity publication of strategies and teaching methods for making spelling as straightforward, accessible and memorable as possible. https://helenarkell.org.uk/product/anyone-can-spell-it

Audio books – There are a variety of audio books libraries including Oxford Owl, an online free e-book library with text and audio publications. www.oxfordowl.co.uk

Barrington Stoke – Publisher of dyslexia-friendly fiction books designed to ensure an accessible but age-appropriate read for weaker readers. https://collins.co.uk/pages/barrington-stoke

British Dyslexia Association New Technologies Committee (BDA NTC) – Information on the latest technology and applications (hardware and software) that may support dyslexic learners. This includes information on text-to-speech software. https://bdanewtechnologies.wordpress.com

Brooks's What Works for Literacy Difficulties? The Effectiveness of Intervention Schemes, 6th Edition – Review intervention schemes available in the UK to support learners struggling to acquire literacy skills. www.theschoolpsychologyservice.com/what-works-for-literacy-difficulties-6th-edition

Easy Spelling Aid – An app designed for iOS (iPhone and iPad) and Android (phone and tablet) that provides a single-word spelling or a whole sentence for any word/s dictated into the microphone. This includes both UK and US spelling. www.easyspellingaid.com

Helen Arkell Auditory Tests (HAAT) – Useful battery of informal, criterion-referenced tests to assess phonological awareness skills and phonic knowledge. Suggestions about activities to encourage auditory and phonological awareness skills. https://helenarkell.org.uk

High Frequency Words – Printable lists of the first 100 and next 200 high frequency words arranged in order of their frequently in English prose. www.highfrequencywords.org

Reader pens – These are hand-held devices intended for weaker readers that read aloud an unfamiliar word or sentence. Some versions may be used in examinations. There is a variety of products available including those from www.scanningpens.co.uk

School Spelling Dictionary – Dyslexia-friendly dictionary published by Barrington Stoke with words arranged according to initial phonic pattern. https://collins.co.uk/collections/barrington-stoke

Spelling Stories – Multisensory resource book by Val Hammond that tells a memorable story for each phonic pattern and then contains photocopiable resources for learners to practise spelling (and reading) each pattern. https://helenarkell.org.uk/product/spelling-stories/#:~:text=Description,spelling%20problems%20such%20as%20dyslexia

Spelling Window – A Helen Arkell Dyslexia Charity product that is a simple, re-usable and very effective multisensory resource for practising spelling single words. https://helenarkell.org.uk

Target Reading Accuracy – A Helen Arkell Dyslexia Charity publication of practical strategies and teaching tools to improve reading accuracy. https://helenarkell.org.uk

Target Reading Comprehension – A Helen Arkell Dyslexia Charity publication of practical tips and activities to improve reading comprehension. https://helenarkell.org.uk

Toe by Toe: A Highly Structured Multi-Sensory Reading Manual for Teachers and Parents supports weaker readers acquire reading accuracy with both phonics and irregular word reading. The book also includes a strategy for reading unfamiliar multisyllabic words. https://toe-by-toe.co.uk

Tricky Spellings in Cartoons – A range of books by Lidia Stanton that provide memorable and fun cartoons to explain the spelling of so many tricky irregular words. https://lidiastanton.com

Worksheet Genius – Free, printable, differentiated and personalised literacy worksheets including precision teaching templates, flashcards, pairs games, etc. https://worksheetgenius.com

REFERENCES

Augur, J. (1985) Guidelines for Teachers, Parents and Learners. In M.J. Snowling (ed.), *Children's Written Language Difficulties: Assessment and Management*. Windsor: NFER-Nelson.

Carroll, J., Holden, C., Kirby, P., Thompson, P.A. and Snowling, M.J. (2025) Toward a consensus on dyslexia: findings from a Delphi study. *Journal of Child Psychology and Psychiatry, 66*(7): 1065–1076.

Cowling, K. and Cowling, H. (1993) *Toe by Toe, A Highly Structured Multi-Sensory Reading Manual for Teachers and Parents*. West Yorkshire: K. and H. Cowling.

Gibby-Leversuch, R., Hartwell, B. and Wright, S. (2021) Dyslexia, literacy difficulties and the self-perceptions of children and young people: a systematic review. *Current Psychology, 40*: 5595–5612.

Lavan, G. and Talcott, J. (ed.) (2020) *Brooks's What Works for Literacy Difficulties? The Effectiveness of Intervention Schemes*, 6th Edition. Available at: www.theschoolpsychologyservice.com/what-works-for-literacy-difficulties-6th-edition

Muter, V. (2021) *Understanding and Supporting Children with Literacy Difficulties: An Evidence-Based Guide for Practitioners*. London: Jessica Kingsley.

INDEX

affixes 49
areas of strength 71
assistive technology
   reading 36–37
   spelling 50
attention deficit hyperactivity
   disorder (ADHD) 3, 5, 6
audio books 17, 37, 77
auditory discrimination 31
auditory methods of learning/
   teaching 17–18
Augur, J. 15
autistic spectrum condition/
   disorder (ASC/ASD) 5, 6
automaticity
   chunking 61
   definition 58
   difficulty achieving 59–60
   plenaries 61
   practising new skills 61
   recapping 60
   scaffolding 61
   steps to 61
   support in developing 60–62

block capitals, avoidance of 26
bold font 26
books
   audio 17, 37, 77
   dyslexia-friendly range of 36
   monitor reading of 36
British Dyslexia Association,
   technology website 37, 77
BUG method 39
bypass strategies, spelling 48–49, 54

case studies
   reading 40
   spelling 54
   verbal instructions 27
   writing 54
chunking 24, 40, 46, 61, 73
   see also segmentation, sounds
   and words
clapping 31
collaboration through talking 17
collages 17
colour
   cards 18
   displays 17
   paper 26
   rainbow writing 47
   visual learning 16
common exception words
   34, 46
complex tasks 24
confidence
   boosting 70–73
   impact of dyslexia on 9, 66
   impact of low 68–69
   recognising low 67
   risk of low 67–68
connectives 53
creative writing, memorable
   strategy 51
curriculum words 38, 49

developmental coordination
   disorder (DCD) 3, 4, 5, 6
developmental language disorder
   (DLD) 3, 5, 6

diagrams 17
  Lotus 52
dictionary, dyslexia-friendly for spelling 50, 78
double meanings, avoiding 24
dyscalculia 3, 4, 5, 6
dysgraphia 4, 5, 6
dyslexia
  characteristic areas of difficulty 6–8
  continuum of difficulties 8
  definitions 2–3
  impact on learning 8–10
  specific learning difficulty 4
dyspraxia *see* developmental coordination disorder

effort, acknowledge and rewarding 72

feedback
  boosting self-esteem 70, 72
  marking 72
  physical 18
  sensitive 67
  verbal 27
flow charts
  visual learning 17
  writing skills 52
fluency, dyslexia impact on 8, 59–60
fonts 26

games and movement 18
graphemes 32, 45

idioms, avoiding 24
independence
  reading skills 35–38
  spelling skills 48–50
irregular words 34–35

multisensory methods in learning 47
  support in spelling 46–47
italic font, avoidance of 26

justified text 26

kinaesthetic methods of learning/teaching 18

language, appropriate
  case study 27
  definition 22–23
  using 22–25
learning objective 62
  achievable 72
letter/sound link cards 33
line spacing 26
long-term memory 15–16
Lotus diagram 52
lower case letters 26

manipulatives and props 18
marking, positive feedback from 72
Matthew effect 35
memorable strategy, creative writing 51
metacognition 73–74
mind maps 52, 71
mistakes, learning from 73
  see also self-correction skills
mnemonics
  auditory method of learning/teaching 18
  support for spelling 46–47, 73
monitor books read 36
Montessori, Maria 15
motivation, lack of 67, 69
multisensory teaching
  auditory methods 17–18

current use of 14
definition 15
kinaesthetic methods 18
reason for 15–16
support in spelling 47
visual methods 16–17

neurodiversity 4–6, 15, 71
  umbrella term 6

Open Dyslexic font 26
orthographic skills 7, 10

paired reading 37, 39
paragraph formation 52
personal spelling journal
  49, 54, 61
phoneme frames 46
phonemes 7, 31, 32
phonic code 32
phonic patterns 33, 34, 45, 46
phonological awareness 3, 7, 30
  Helen Arkell Tests 78
  Spelling Stories (resource
    book) 78
  supporting 31–32
  weak 9
phonological processing 3, 7
  awareness 7, 9
  decoding skill 7, 10
  memory 7, 10
  speed 7, 9, 10, 23, 38
pictures 16–17
planning creative writing
  51–52
plenaries 61
positive experiences 71–72
positive language 23, 25
post-it notes 16
practical demonstration, visual
  learning 17

practical work, kinaesthetic
  method of learning and
  teaching 18
predictive/corrective text 49–50
processing speed, phonological
  3, 7, 9, 10
proofreading 53
punctuation pyramid 53

rainbow writing 47
raps 17
reader pens 37, 61
reading 29–41
  case study 40
  developing skills and
    independence 35–38
  lack of fluency 59
  phonological awareness 31–32
  supporting early skills 32–35
  see also reading comprehension
reading aloud, technology and
  17, 36–37
  see also audio books; reader
    pens
reading comprehension 38–39
  automaticity and 60
  case study 40
reading skills
  dyslexia impact on 8
  supporting development of
    35–38
recap previous learning 60
recording own voice 17
regular words 33–34
  support in spelling 45–46
repeat out loud 17
repeated reading 38
repeating information 25
repetition/practise of new skills
  60–61
resilience, boosting self-esteem 73

rhyme(s)
  auditory method of learning/teaching 17
  sound patterns in words 32
root words 49
rules 47–48

sarcasm, avoiding 24
scaffolding
  practising new skills 61
  writing skills 52–53
scanning 39
  see also reader pens
secondary school, subject knowledge and vocabulary required 30, 38, 48
segmentation, sounds and words 32, 46
self-correction skills 36, 53
self-esteem, low 9
self-esteem and confidence 65–75
  boosting 70–73
  definition 66
  impact of low 68–69
  recognising low 67
  risk of low 67–68
self-monitoring 36
senses, multisensory approach to learning 15–16
sentence starters 53
sequential instructions 24
shared reading 37
sight words 33, 34, 46
signal words 23, 24
  case study 27
simple instructions 23, 24
skimming 39
soft black text 26
sounds in words 31
  segmentation 32, 46
speaking slowly 23

specific learning difficulties 4–6
speech-to-text applications 36–37, 50, 77
  case study 54
spelling
  automaticity and 60
  cartoons 79
  case study 54
  developing skills 48–50
  dictionary 78
  Easy Spelling Aid app 77–78
  irregular words 46–47
  personal spelling journal 49, 54, 61
  regular words 45–46
  stories 78
  window 78
  words following rules 47–48
spelling patterns 31–34, 45–46, 48
standing up 18
sticky notes, planning creative writing 52
story mountains 52
subvocalising 17
  irregular words 47
  regular words 46
suffixes 49

talk
  collaboration through 17
  stop when/whilst child working 23–24
  see also language, appropriate
targets, achievable 72
technology *see* text-to-speech applications
text-to-speech applications 17, 36–37, 50, 61, 77
  case study 54
thinking time 23

underlining font, avoidance of 26
understanding, checking 25
unfamiliar patterns, word families 33

video 17, 25
visual difficulties 7–8
visual display, boost for self-esteem/confidence 72–73
visual methods of learning/teaching 16–17

WAGOLL (what a good one looks like) 25
word attack strategy 34
  case study 40
word mat 53
word processors 49–50, 52
  case study 54
working memory 3, 7, 10, 23, 34, 38, 45, 46, 50, 52, 59
Worksheet Genius (website) 34, 79
WOW
  wall 72
  words 53
writing
  case studies 27, 54
  dysgraphia 5
  supporting 50–53
written resources, presentation style 25–26